REPOSSESSED

Greg Lam

BROADWAY PLAY PUBLISHING INC
New York
www.broadwayplaypublishing.com
info@broadwayplaypublishing.com

REPOSSESSED

Cover art courtesy of Theatre Conspiracy

First edition: April 2023
I S B N: 978-0-88145-981-4

Book design: Marie Donovan
Page make-up: Adobe InDesign
Typeface: Palatino

An early version of REPOSSESSED was developed and presented at Pork Filled Productions in Seattle. It was further developed and presented at Fresh Ink Theatre, Boston.

REPOSSESSED received its world premiere at Theatre Conspiracy (Bill Taylor, Artistic Director) in Fort Myers, Florida running from 16-26 August 2018. The cast and creative contributors were:

GRETCHEN WARNER..................................Rachel Burttram
RICH WARNER ....Brendan Powers
TED NAUGHTON ....Patrick Day
REGINA HASTINGS.......................................Lauren Drexler
CINDY ....Tamicka Armstrong
VOICE...Joann Haley
other roles..................................Lisa Kuchinski, Tom Short

Director...Stephen Hooper
Stage Manager..June Koc
Set design..Bill Taylor
Technical Director ....Curtis Jones

CHARACTERS

RICH WARNER, 45. *Appears to be a charming self-possessed man of dignity and success, used to being a success at all levels of life, like someone who has just finished giving his Ted Talk.*

GRETCHEN WARNER, 35. *Appears to be a cultured and intelligent woman of style and tact, like someone just featured in* The New York Times *Style section.*

REGINA HASTINGS, 50. *Appears to be an ambitious and powerful woman heading a groundbreaking biotech company, like someone who just nailed her Senate testimony.*

TED NAUGHTON, 55. *A lawyer and* RICH*'s longtime friend despite his obvious shortcomings.*

CINDY, 28. *Appears to be just a girl you meet but don't really think much about.*

Other small roles, as assigned to two additional actors:

Actor 1:
SERVER
NURSE
SURGEON 1
REGINA'S ASSISTANT
DOORMAN

Actor 2:
SURGEON 2
RESTAURANT PATRON

CONFERENCE HOST
THE VOICE

With the doubling as noted, the play can be produced with a minimum of seven actors.

The play can be done without an act break. If you want to perform the play with an act break, you may do so with the act break inserted after Scene 12. In that case, move Interlude 4 to the top of ACT TWO.

AUTHOR'S NOTE

This play has scenes set in the present day and flashback scenes set in the past. The present-day scenes take place in a linear fashion, timewise. Flashback scenes are *not* inserted in a linear chronological order. These scenes should be presented in a different manner than the present day scenes, probably through lighting design and sound design.

As we have many transitions between time and place in this play, the scenes should be rendered as minimally as possible to make the transitions nimble.

Café Nuance is a fake restaurant run by LifeEnhanced where they can stage interactions in a public seeming controlled environment as needed, monitored by the LifeEnhanced staff. The staff and many of the other patrons are LifeEnhanced employees who observe enhanced customers during their post enhancement interactions and intervene if necessary.

The overall point to all of this is that LifeEnhanced is an established, well-thought out, mature company that has come up with various methods to make some difficult operations work. These aren't all of the methods they use to keep their customers on track, but they're the ones that apply to this situation.

Scene 1
Café Nuance

(At rise: The interior of Café Nuance, a well-appointed upscale restaurant. The type of place you'd go on a nice Friday night out, but probably not for an anniversary.)

*(*GRETCHEN *sits, holding a glass of wine and scanning the restaurant.)*

(A SERVER *enters.)*

SERVER: Miss? Can I get anything for you while you wait?

GRETCHEN: Hmmm? Oh, no thank you. I'm fine.

SERVER: Of course. If you change your mind, just let me know.

(The SERVER *leaves.* GRETCHEN *sips her wine.)*

(From a doorway, RICH, *45, enters. He is* GRETCHEN*'s husband, a tech entrepreneur. He wears a crisp shirt, sleeves rolled up. He's graying a bit, and is just on the edge of being out of shape.)*

*(*RICH *sees his wife before she sees him. He takes a moment to compose himself.)*

RICH: Starting without me?

GRETCHEN: You know me. Can't resist a good Riesling. And here's your drink.

*(*GRETCHEN *hands* RICH *a glass of water. They clink their glasses together and take a sip.)*

(*The* MAITRE'D *seats another couple.*)

RICH: Hmmm. Tap water. A wonderful vintage.

GRETCHEN: I'm so glad we decided to go out tonight. We deserve a good night. The way things have been… Who knows if we'll be able to go out like this a year from now?

RICH: Gretchen—

GRETCHEN: Oh, I didn't mean- I just wanted to savor little things like date night with my husband before things change.

RICH: I'm sorry. My decision to close the company wasn't taken lightly.

GRETCHEN: We'll be alright.

RICH: Of course we will.

GRETCHEN: It's only money.

RICH: Gretchen. Are you okay with this? Or are you just putting on a brave face?

GRETCHEN: Of course I'm okay.

RICH: It's a lot to ask of you.

GRETCHEN: You didn't have much of a choice.

RICH: Of course I did. We always have choice. Just imagine that there are two buttons before you that you could press—

GRETCHEN: (*Gently teasing*) Again with your brain teasers!

RICH: It's how I think. Take complex situations and break it into smaller, more manageable units using hypotheticals.

GRETCHEN: I'll play along.

RICH: Alright. Two buttons. Press the first button: Where we are now. The company closes and we take a big hit in the wallet. Press the second button: We go back in time. I swallow my pride and go back to my old job. Sell off our company's assets as best I can. I've had offers from other game companies. They've made pitches about what parts of the game are worth saving and what should be thrown out. If I could stand to watch them take my baby and turn it into sausage, we'd have enough money to maintain our lifestyle.

GRETCHEN: I would never ask you to compromise yourself.

RICH: I know. But I would do that for you. So, two buttons. Which do you press?

GRETCHEN: The first button, of course. It's not even a question. Would I ask you to sell yourself out? We could maintain some illusion of success but you'd be dying inside. Who would ask such a thing?

RICH: Some wives might.

GRETCHEN: Well, not this one.

RICH: I knew I married the right woman.

*(*GRETCHEN *and* RICH *kiss.)*

RICH: Once we sell the house, we'll have a little breathing space. And we can enjoy our cozy apartment.

GRETCHEN: That will be nice.

RICH: And we start over. There are some VCs who will still take my call.

GRETCHEN: And I'll get a job. I hear the market is positively booming for people with a Master's in 19th century French literature and no recent work experience.

*(*RICH *laughs.)*

RICH: Before I forget, Ted asked us to stop by his office tomorrow.

GRETCHEN: Both of us? Why does your lawyer need me?

RICH: Not sure, but he said we should both be there. Made me promise to bring you.

GRETCHEN: Why would he ask that?

RICH: Gretchen—

GRETCHEN: I know. I know. He's one of your oldest friends. But after all this time I… I still don't know if he likes me.

RICH: Of course he does. Who wouldn't? Who wouldn't like the perfect woman?

*(*GRETCHEN *smiles. The* SERVER *returns.)*

SERVER: Welcome to Café Nuance. Have you made your decisions tonight, or do you need more time?

Scene 2
Meeting room

(The meeting room of a high-end law firm.)

(At the table, a woman in an immaculate suit waits. She is REGINA HASTINGS, *50. She regards herself in the mirror, making sure every detail is in place.)*

(Then she just waits.)

(A man in a very badly fitting suit enters, followed by RICH *and* GRETCHEN. *The man in the suit is* TED NAUGHTON, *55, a lawyer.)*

TED: …just a bunch of sons of bitches. I don't mind telling you that. Every time I hear someone taking shots at you it sends me through the fucking roof. Your company deserved better. You deserved better, bud.

RICH: Even the best startups have risks involved. I knew what I was getting into.

TED: Every video game nerd I could find has told me that this game of yours would have been great, if the funding had come through.

RICH: Luck was not on our side.

TED: Well, as your lawyer, and your friend. If there's anything I can do. Y'know?

RICH: Thanks. We have enough socked away to weather the worst of it. It'll be an adjustment but…

GRETCHEN: I meant it when I said "For richer or poorer."

TED: That's great, great to hear. My first wife said that, too! Too bad she didn't mean it!

*(*TED *laughs at his own joke. He's the only one laughing.)*

*(*REGINA *speaks.)*

REGINA: And should I introduce myself, Mr Naughton?

RICH: Oh, I'm sorry. Was this conference room taken?

TED: No, Regina—Miss Hastings. Mrs? Miz?

REGINA: Regina.

TED: I invited her to meet with us. Regina, this is Rich and Gretchen Warner.

REGINA: Pleasure to meet you both.

(They exchange handshakes.)

TED: Regina is from a company you might have heard of. Been in the news a bit lately. "LifeEnhanced".

RICH: I don't think I have.

GRETCHEN: LifeEnhanced? Oh, I read about you in *The New Yorker* a few months ago. Fascinating company.

REGINA: I'm glad our reputation precedes us, though that particular article painted us in a bit of an alarmist light.

RICH: Oh, right. You're the company that helps people quit smoking and lose weight.

GRETCHEN: Oh, it's much more interesting than that. They change minds.

RICH: I'm sorry?

GRETCHEN: I mean, they can implant things like skills and experiences into you, directly into your brain, surgically. If you always wanted to be a great musician, they could upload a virtuoso's skill into your head and then you could play Tchaikovsky at Carnegie Hall.

RICH: Really? How about some of Tiger Woods' long game?

REGINA: In theory, yes. If we could get Mr Woods to donate his knowledge to our company. And of course your body remains your own. But what can be done to improve your mind, we can do.

RICH: Well, while I could use some help here or there, I don't imagine your services come cheap.

REGINA: No, they don't. Only a very few people can afford our services. Especially for our *Vita Totalis* package.

RICH: "Vita Totalis" package?

GRETCHEN: Latin for "Total Life".

REGINA: That's what we call our total life makeovers at LifeEnhanced. Instead of adding one or two skills to your arsenal, we can completely refurbish a person's life. Make her a new person. We could take a soldier with PTSD and upload a boring, stress-free life into him. We can change a drug addict into a teetotaler, a pornstar into a nun, or vice versa. Whatever you can imagine, we can do.

GRETCHEN: Remarkable. I didn't know you could go that far.

REGINA: Yes, we don't tend to publicize that. It's a bit far reaching for some at the moment. The only people that really need to know are the prospective customers.

RICH: Well, now we get to it. Miss Hastings, if you're here to sell your services, I'm afraid we're not in the market. As much as I'd like some help with my golf game, right now our finances aren't in any shape to cooperate. So, thanks for the fascinating pitch, but I have some pressing matters to discuss with my lawyer.

TED: Well, Rich, the thing is…Regina is the pressing matter we have to discuss right now. She's not here to sell you on her company's services. You've actually been a client of theirs for some time now.

GRETCHEN: You have?

REGINA: For five years now, Mr Warner.

GRETCHEN: You never told me.

RICH: I…I don't know what they're talking about.

REGINA: He didn't know, Mrs Warner. Our agreement was that he wouldn't be aware of the changes that he requested for himself. It's common for makeovers of this magnitude for the recipient to be unaware that he's had work done. Per our agreement Mr Naughton acted as the monitor and proxy to his situation.

RICH: Ted?

TED: It's true, Rich.

RICH: This is quite the tale. Not what I expected when you asked us here for a meeting. So what did I get? It can't be my golf game, I'll tell you that much.

REGINA: You were actually one of the first buyers of our *Totalis* packages. A complete life makeover. Seamless integration into your previous persona. You wake up one day with a different life, and you don't even know it. It was something of a proof of concept for our company, and it succeeded magnificently.

RICH: I'm sorry, but what do you mean by "It"? What succeeded?

REGINA: Your marriage. We created it. You and Gretchen had never met before we put you together, at your request. We uploaded two years of relationship into each of your brains.

*(*RICH *and* GRETCHEN *look at each other, chilled.)*

REGINA: I'm sorry to be the one who has to tell you.

GRETCHEN: I don't know what this is but this is insane.

TED: It's the truth, I'm sorry to say. It's all true.

*(*TED *presses a button. Offstage a video screen plays. They all look.* RICH *and* GRETCHEN *are surprised at what they see.)*

TED: They insisted that they film your consenting to the implants.

REGINA: Part of our standard procedures Mr Naughton helped us devise. See Mr Warner? We have met before.

RICH: It looks like me. A little younger. But I have no memory of this. Why would I do this?

TED: It's mostly my fault. You were so goddamn mopey after Diana dumped you and I heard about this company. You needed someone stable in your life but you were killing yourself with your work. You were never going to find a chick who… well… You know.

GRETCHEN: No, I don't know, Ted. What was he not going to find?

REGINA: Someone who deserved him. Richard was in need of companionship of the highest quality, but he did not have the werewithal to find it via the traditional methods. Our company offered an alternative solution.

GRETCHEN: You said "two years of relationship" were uploaded. I broke my leg skiing in Aspen and he waited on me hand and foot for a month. Are you serious? And… and going to my mother's funeral? That was at the beginning, too. *(She turns to* RICH.*)* I cried all night in your arms, and I realized that we would be together forever. And that wasn't real?

REGINA: Those are real experiences, but they each happened to someone else before we gave them to you. Those repurposed memories are more convincing than wholly manufactured experiences, we've found. You get the right little details you just can't get otherwise, once we nudge them into place.

GRETCHEN: Rich only shaved half his face that day. He stopped when I started crying and never got back to it until the next day. All fake?

REGINA: You came to us as strangers and when we were finished you were a well matched couple very much in love.

GRETCHEN: I didn't even know him? This is preposterous. Why did I agree to this? Who- Who would do that?

*(*REGINA *presses a button. A new video plays.)*

REGINA: Who? You were a young, pretty woman who decided that being married to a rich man that you didn't know was better than the life you had been leading.

GRETCHEN: That's me? What the hell am I wearing?

RICH: Baby—

GRETCHEN: Don't. Don't touch me. This is sick. If this is true, this means our whole life is a lie. Look at the screen, that's me with electrodes in my head. Probably getting our first time in bed together implanted in my brain.

RICH: I don't care about this. I love you, no matter how we got here. We'll get through this. We can do it. Come here.

(They hug desperately.)

GRETCHEN: It still feels like you.

RICH: Ted, there better be a good reason that you're telling us this.

TED: Afraid there is, bud.

RICH: Well, no time like the present. What's the deal?

TED: So, when we arranged all this, you paid the down payment, and then we also set up the subscription that paid for the yearly maintenance fee.

RICH: "Maintenance"?

REGINA: Periodically, we would check in on you for a reconcilation procedure. Sometimes the reality you were given doesn't match the reality that you perceive, and we need to smooth over those rough patches to maintain the effect using a variety of procedures ranging from phone calls to physical interactions to surgical upgrades. If that regimen isn't kept up with, some inconvenient side effects are felt. Anxiety, paranoia, depression. It's quite a vital part of the process.

TED: So long as you kept up with the subscription fees, you'd be able to keep the implanted reality fully intact throughout your lifetimes.

RICH: So… With our finances in the crapper…

TED: Yeah. It was my call. As your trustee, and with your recent troubles, I thought it was better to keep a roof over your heads than to keep this up.

RICH: You really believe that?

TED: I've seen your financials.

REGINA: And I agreed with Mr Naughton's decision. It's best for you both if our company were to uninstall our enhancements.

GRETCHEN: You're taking this, whatever "this" is, away?

REGINA: Yes. Your upgrades will be removed, surgically. Your false memories will fade and be supplanted by your actual memories of that time period resurfacing. The actual memories you've accrued since the procedure are yours to keep, however.

GRETCHEN: Thank heavens for small favors, I suppose.

REGINA: It's not ideal, Mrs Warner, but it's the contract that all parties agreed to. If it makes you feel better, we no longer do things like this. Now we require the full lifetime payment up front.

GRETCHEN: Our marriage…is that fake, too?

TED: Oh, you're still legally married. That happened. I was there. You're just, you know, going to lose a few things.

REGINA: Yes, Richard couldn't marry just anyone. He wanted someone he could talk to and who could easily be around the friends and social circle of a rising entrepreneur. So we implanted in you a college education, Master's degree, interest in photography and poetry, debutante training. Ability to speak French. That one you got from me.

TED: So that's going away. A lot of little odds and ends that make you into the…uh…

REGINA: The wonderful woman that you are.

TED: Yeah. Classy shit and stuff.

GRETCHEN: Then what's left? Who am I when all that's gone?

RICH: And what about me? What do I stand to lose?

TED: You got some things that make you a bit better in a relationship. Maturity, patience, emotional stability. Let's be frank. You were a train wreck when this happened. Made running a business kind of inconvenient.

GRETCHEN: And he'll be like that again?

REGINA: Not necessarily. In the very few instances in which we've had implants rescinded, it's not unusual to have some level of developed talents and traits remain. Richard is a rather good husband from what I've heard.

GRETCHEN: He's a perfect husband. Perfect.

REGINA: It wouldn't surprise me if he retains at least some of that. Skills develop. Lessons are learned. Even tastes change.

GRETCHEN: Is that what you think will happen?

REGINA: It's not impossible.

GRETCHEN: But not probable. Is that what you mean, Miss Hastings?

RICH: Baby—

GRETCHEN: Don't "Baby" me, Rich. Why are you just standing there? You're still going to be able to make another company, another fortune. What am I going back to? Apparently I had nothing going on in my life if I agreed to this. What am I? A prostitute?

RICH: Baby, please. Listen to me. Whatever brought us together, I have no regrets. You are the best thing to ever happen to me. And I am bound and determined that whatever happens next, I will not let you go. We will survive this.

GRETCHEN: Oh, Rich. I want to believe you. But what if the part of you that said that is the part that gets taken out?

TED: Look, guys, it's a lot to absorb, I know. I think we should leave you two alone for a bit so you can process. I worked it out with Regina and you can have another month before they have to begin the procedures. So…

RICH: Okay, Ted. Thanks.

TED: Good luck, Bud.

RICH: Hey Ted?

TED: Yeah?

RICH: I seem to recall that about six or seven years ago is when I quit drinking.

TED: Yeah. Sounds about right. Real proud of you for that.

RICH: Well, it has to be asked. Did I do that all by myself?

(Pause)

TED: How do you want me to answer that, Rich?

RICH: You just did, Ted. Goodbye.

*(*TED *exits.)*

REGINA: Well, it was wonderful to meet you both again. Really, I wish I didn't have to be the one… It's just business.

*(*REGINA *exits.* GRETCHEN *and* RICH *look at one another. Eventually they settle on holding hands. They look at the screen.)*

GRETCHEN: Look at us, Rich. Is that our first meeting? We don't even know each other.

RICH: I know.

GRETCHEN: Look at me. I'm acting like the vacuous bubbleheaded bimbos I always look down on.

RICH: No you aren't.

GRETCHEN: No manners, no posture. I'm dressed like a trollop. And do I have a tattoo? I do! I suppose you liked that. What the hell was going on in my life that this seemed like a good idea?

RICH: Hey, c'mon. The last five years. With me. Remember? We did those things. We will remember them.

*(*GRETCHEN *and* RICH *hug.)*

GRETCHEN: This feels so real.

RICH: It is real.

GRETCHEN: Is it?

Scene 3
LifeEnhanced labs (flashback)

(The lights turn on. We see TED *and* REGINA *in a conference room. A window looks out into another room through one-way glass.)*

*(*TED *is sorting through headshots of women.)*

(This scene is set in an earlier time period than the previous scenes. Those scenes should be presented differently than the "present day" scenes, visually.)

TED: Jesus Christ. How many more do we have to see? All this work to get someone else some action.

REGINA: Candidate 7 is the last we've asked to see today. If you find none of the candidates are adequate, we can recruit more candidates. All part of what our company can offer.

TED: For what we're paying? We'd better be able to see every hot goldigger in the state to pick from.

REGINA: Well, I'm not sure we can promise that, Mr Naughton. At least not yet. But I think you'll like Candidate 7.

TED: Let's take a look.

*(*REGINA *presses a button.)*

(The lights go up to reveal GRETCHEN, *now dressed only in a sports bra and yoga shorts. Her posture is slouched, her manner is jittery and youthful. She sways back and forth nervously. She's five years younger. There's a sign pinned to her shorts with a number printed on it: "7". She stands blinded by bright lights.)*

*(*TED *studies her through the glass.)*

TED: Huh. Now, that's a bit of allright.

REGINA: Is she his type?

TED: She's anyone's type. She's definitely my type.

*(*REGINA *speaks into a microphone. Her voice is amplified so that* GRETCHEN *can hear it.)*

REGINA: *(Amplified)* Good afternoon.

*(*GRETCHEN *is a bit startled by the sudden noise. When she speaks, her accent is different. Lower status/class.)*

GRETCHEN: Hi?

REGINA: *(Amplified)* Please try to relax. We only wish to ask a few questions.

GRETCHEN: Okay. This is kind of weird.

REGINA: *(Amplified)* I know, but please bear with us. And thank you for participating in our candidate screening procedure. Candidate 7, can you restate, in your own words, what brings you here?

GRETCHEN: Uh… The 49 bus?

REGINA: *(Amplified)* No, I meant something a bit different. The procedure we have proposed is quite new, some might say extreme. Definitely life-altering. We want for you to state, for the record, why you've decided to make yourself a candidate for this.

GRETCHEN: Well, I don't know. I'm just… It's exciting? I mean, I dropped out of college to follow my boyfriend across the country. So that didn't last, obviously. Neither has any other relationship. You know how it is. I never went back to school. I burnt bridges. I'm not good at work. I get jobs. I do them, they're fine. But they're just jobs. It's not like I love anything I do. So why not?

REGINA: *(Amplified)* Do you think becoming altered to become someone's ideal partner is better?

GRETCHEN: I don't know. I'm almost thirty, and I have no idea what I want to do with my life. Like, none. I don't belong. I guess I'd like to be somewhere that felt like I belonged.

REGINA: *(Amplified)* Does it matter that you don't know him?

GRETCHEN: I don't know. What do you want me to say? You're going to put into my head whatever, right? So what does it matter? As long as his checks clear.

REGINA: *(Amplified)* I see.

GRETCHEN: He's not hideous, right?

REGINA: *(Amplified)* In my opinion, he's more than adequate.

GRETCHEN: I'm sorry. That's too mean. I'm really nervous right now if you can't tell. I know I don't get to choose the guy. That's not how it works. I know that. When I think about it. if the guy is going to go to the trouble of making me into his dream girl, what are the chances he wouldn't treat me right? Pretty low, right?

REGINA: *(Amplified)* I don't know the answer to that question.

GRETCHEN: I know. It wasn't meant to be answered. It's, whatdyacallit?

REGINA: *(Amplified)* Rhetorical?

GRETCHEN: That's it. Someone who'll treat me right, no matter what. That's harder to find than you'd think.

REGINA: *(Amplified)* Agreed.

*(*REGINA *turns to* TED.*)*

REGINA: Anything you'd like to ask her?

TED: Sure.

*(*TED *speaks into the microphone.)*

TED: *(Amplified)* Hey number 7. This is Ted. I'm the guy helping my bud choose a girl to go through the process.

GRETCHEN: OK. Nice to "meet" you, Ted.

TED: *(Amplified)* Yeah, yeah. Could you turn around?

Gretchen quickly twists to look behind her.

TED: *(Amplified)* No, I meant. Turn around. All of you. Slowly.

*(*GRETCHEN *starts to turn. She has a butterfly tattoo at the small of her back.)*

TED: *(Amplified)* Let's just get a good long look at what we're working with. I like the tramp stamp, honey.

*(*GRETCHEN *gets more and more uncomfortable. She completes her turn.)*

TED: *(Amplified)* Very nice. Now can you dance a little?

*(*REGINA *shuts off the microphone.)*

REGINA: Mr Naughton! For God's sake, this isn't a strip club.

GRETCHEN: Are… Are you serious?

TED: For the amount of cash we're dropping, I'd expect that chick to give me a lap dance with a happy ending. Heck, for what we're paying I'd expect that from you, too.

GRETCHEN: Hello? Is this a test? Do I have to dance? I don't really do that.

REGINA: Please finish up, Mr Naughton.

TED: *(Amplified)* You're done, sweetheart. You look good to me.

GRETCHEN: Can I go now?

REGINA: *(Amplified)* Yes. Thank you candidate 7. We'll be in touch.

Scene 4
Regina's office

*(*REGINA *sits at her desk.* RICH *enters.)*

REGINA: Mr Warner.

RICH: Ms Hastings. Thank you for agreeing to meet with me.

REGINA: All part of a day's work. What can I do for you?

RICH: I've been thinking about a lot of things recently, looking into this company more, as much as I can glean from the few real information sources available.

REGINA: We like to keep a low profile, for now.

RICH: I have to say that what you're doing is quite impressive, and also not too far out of line with my work. As a game designer, I've built a career of making virtual playgrounds for people to spend time in. You turn reality into a virtual playground. That's how I've come to see it.

REGINA: A very clever insight.

RICH: I've also been thinking about whether there are any options that we might have to avoid the upcoming messiness of our reversions. My wife and I are obviously quite attached to our current personas.

REGINA: And what were you thinking exactly?

RICH: Well, what if I were to lend my talents to your company in exchange for a continued subcription to our maintenance? You must know the reputation my software has had in terms of creative vision and imagination. A lot of what was a key strength for my games was narrative cohesion and world building. That would certainly be transferable when talking about what your company does.

REGINA: I see. It's an interesting offer, but I think we'd have to decline.

RICH: But you haven't even heard my ideas—

REGINA: It's alright, Mr Warner.

RICH: Will you dismiss me summarily? I was about to rewrite the future of my field.

REGINA: Having you as a client means that we've made an extensive inventory of what's already in your mind and your level of capability, both current and potential.

And what you have right now is not unique to what we have in our database.

RICH: I see.

REGINA: If we wanted a "you" it'd probably be easier to make one.

RICH: Alright. It's your loss.

REGINA: I agree. Now, since we have you here, let me discuss the offboarding procedure with you in a bit more detail. Shall we go over some options?

Scene 5
Café Nuance

(A table for two. Present day)

*(*GRETCHEN *and* RICH *sit at the usual table. A* SERVER *finishes telling them about the specials.)*

SERVER: …and last we have a pan seared salmon with scalloped potatoes. Served with a hollandaise dill sauce and asparagus. Well, I'll let you think about it for a while and then I'll take your order.

(The SERVER *then leaves, leaving* RICH *and* GRETCHEN *alone to stare idly at the menu. She looks at him.)*

GRETCHEN: So… What are we going to do?

RICH: I was thinking the pork chop special sounded good.

GRETCHEN: I'm sorry?

RICH: Garlic mashed potatoes with gorgonzola? Come on!

GRETCHEN: Rich, for God's sake. Can you be serious about this?

RICH: I guess you don't mean dinner, then.

(The MAITRE'D *seats another couple. The same people as the previous scene in the café.)*

GRETCHEN: We have a week, just one week before we have to return our- our brains to the brain shop. What do we do?

RICH: I don't know.

GRETCHEN: You're supposed to know, Rich. And I'm supposed to follow you around staring adoringly into your eyes. Wasn't that the deal?

RICH: I believe so.

GRETCHEN: What is going to happen to us?

RICH: Do you hate me?

GRETCHEN: No. My God. I hate myself.

RICH: You mustn't. I'm at fault for all of this. You had nothing to do with this.

GRETCHEN: That's what I hate about it. I'm…I'm a prop. I'm a thing. I'm just a piece of merchandise you saw on a shelf and put in your cart. I let you do that. What kind of person would let herself be bought and sold like that?

RICH: But we made you perfect.

GRETCHEN: Well, not anymore! Whatever I was that I was so eager to run away from, I'm heading right back there. Oh, God. What are we going to do?

RICH: Listen, Gretch. Look at me. I'm going to have to go back too. From what I can tell, I was in even worse shape than you were, right? You were a gal looking for a change. Ted says I was a mess that needed help.

GRETCHEN: I can't even imagine that. You've always been so…solid. So sturdy. The earth under my feet.

RICH: I've tried to be that for you. Always. But now…I don't know what's going to happen. We're each going to go in as one person and come out another one. It's really remarkable what they can do, the more I look into it… Sorry. It's the designer in me. I can't help how fascinating it is that they're making designer people.

GRETCHEN: I think it's horrid. I don't want to become someone else. I want to be me.

RICH: Hey, hey. I need you. We said our vows. We really did. As far as I'm concerned, they're still in play. How about you?

GRETCHEN: Yes.

RICH: Then let's do it. Whatever our faults were, we're good people now. Maybe we don't need the help anymore.

GRETCHEN: I wish I believed like you do.

RICH: Hastings said that one of us has to go first, get the… stuff removed. I think I should go first and face the inevitable.

GRETCHEN: You do? You'd do that?

RICH: Of course. And once I show that it can be done, then it'll be a breeze for you. What do you think?

GRETCHEN: I don't know what I think. What in the world am I going back to?

Scene 6
Gretchen's apartment (flashback)

(An energetic young woman named CINDY *[26] enters, holding a case of beer and a plastic bag with DVDs in it. She knocks on the door heavily.)*

CINDY: I know you're in there! *(She knocks again.)* Crystal Schenkman, it's one of your last days on earth as yourself, so I got us a case of something awesome and cheap and three trashy rom coms to properly send you off! So let me in before I blow your house down!

(Younger GRETCHEN *opens the door, wearing her bathrobe.)*

GRETCHEN: Seriously, Cindy?

CINDY: Seriously. I'm not letting your last day go uncelebrated.

GRETCHEN: Fine. Come in.

*(*CINDY *smiles and enters. She makes herself right at home.)*

GRETCHEN: I can't get too wild tonight. My body is no longer mine. That was made perfectly clear to me when I signed the contract. If I get hurt or tattooed or knocked up or whatever before the procedure the whole deal's off. And then I'll even have to repay them for getting my tramp stamp lasered off of my butt.

CINDY: I'm not proposing a bachelorette party or a one night stand with the cute bartender who has always had a crush on you, Schenkman. Just some fine domestic light beer and the best movies from the Meg Ryan catalogue.

GRETCHEN: And another thing. My name won't be Crystal Schenkman, soon.

CINDY: Ooh! Have you chosen your stripper name yet?

GRETCHEN: It's not a stripper name, Cindy. It's an "alternative identity".

CINDY: A what now?

GRETCHEN: That's what they call it. They have, umm… euphemisms for everything at that place. "Alternative Identities", "Cerebral Enhancement Procedures", "Moral Boundary Agreements".

CINDY: "Moral Boundary Agreements"? What is that?

GRETCHEN: Oh God. Those are the things I will and won't do when I become the new me. There was this questionnaire like ten pages long filled with boxes I had to check and blanks I had to fill. Rate this or that on the scale of zero to ten. I blushed all the way through the "Intimate Activities" section. I didn't think I was a prude until I started reading those questions. Some people are into really weird stuff.

CINDY: The guy didn't just order you up like he saw fit?

GRETCHEN: No. There were a few things he wanted that I had to agree to. Nothing big. Like, he wants me to have a Masters degree in something but not want to work. I'm like, okay, whatever. We had to negotiate on when I'd want to have kids from "never" to "maybe ten years from now…one kid!". But mostly they're my decisions with his final approval. It was like I was writing a character in a story. But I know I'm going to become that character.

CINDY: Do you get any say over him?

GRETCHEN: Some. I made him a secret, shameful fan of anyone from the original Lilith Fair lineup just for the hell of it.

CINDY: You didn't!

GRETCHEN: I did. He'll try to hide from me that he knows every lyric to every Indigo Girls song. It'll be so adorable. He signed off on it!

CINDY: Hey. So are you going to miss all this? You're not going to remember any of it.

GRETCHEN: What's to miss? Barely being able to make rent every month? Getting hit on at work by drunks? Not having a future? Growing old alone? Seriously, what's to miss?

(Unseen by GRETCHEN, CINDY *looks sad but hides it from* GRETCHEN *well.)*

CINDY: The guy. Mr Indigo Girls. Do you like him?

GRETCHEN: From what I've seen, he seems fine. Just went through a bad break up, and this is how he's coping. His ex really did a number on him, so now he has all these trust issues. There was a lot in the agreements about how he needs me to stand by him, support him, look out for his needs.

CINDY: That doesn't sound like much fun.

GRETCHEN: But I can totally do that. I can be that wifey. And by the time the head doctors are through with him he won't remember that bitches' name. If he could loosen up a bit… Lose ten, fifteen pounds… Let's just say I've dated worse.

CINDY: I'll say!

GRETCHEN: This is such a bizarre conversation to have, Cin. I can't tell you. You're the only person I can talk to about this.

CINDY: Hey. You won't remember me, but I am going to miss you.

GRETCHEN: I'll be around.

CINDY: No you won't. Not really.

GRETCHEN: I guess not.

CINDY: You're really going through with this?

GRETCHEN: I am. I really am.

CINDY: Then a toast!

*(*CINDY *and* GRETCHEN *both open a can of beer.)*

CINDY: It's goodbye to Crystal Schenkman, hello to… What's your name again?

GRETCHEN: The ever so elegant Gretchen Van Der Pool, soon to be Mrs Gretchen Warner.

*(*CINDY *and* GRETCHEN *clink beer cans.)*

CINDY: To Gretchen!

Interlude 1
Rich's surgery

(Darkness. Beeping and breathy whirring. Then the voices of two SURGEONS *are heard.)*

SURGEON 1: …58…59…60. All signs are stable. We can begin.

SURGEON 2: Turning on the array. On the screen we've located the first area with implanted enhancements. On my mark we will begin extraction with #1.

SURGEON 1: Ready.

SURGEON 2: Begin.

(Sounds fade out.)

Interlude 2
Rich's Tech Talk (flashback)

(A tech conference stage. The kind you might watch on YouTube.)

(A CONFERENCE HOST *stands at a podium on the stage. A business conference atmosphere, trying to project the image of the cutting edge. Well-convinced of their own importance)*

CONFERENCE HOST: …thanks to Professor Smithson. I'll never look at The Import Tax the same way again, I'll tell you that. Now, many of you have waited this entire conference for this. So without further ado, the next Tech Talk speaker, the man making waves and revolutionizing gaming as we know it, founder and CEO of Savage Avatar Games, Richard Warner.

*(*RICH *enters and shakes hands with the* CONFERENCE HOST. *The* CONFERENCE HOST *exits and* RICH *addresses the audience.)*

RICH: "What are you doing, spending your life playing video games?" You've heard that question, haven't you? I know I have, even now. And there's never a good answer for this question, is there? People on the outside of our industry are not usually impressed when we say "gaining experience points so that I can level up and buy a Sword of Triumph". My darling wife, Gretchen, always rolls her eyes at me a bit when I say something like that. "Talk to me when you want to rejoin the real world," she says.

And yet, millions of people choose to spend their time not in the real world where my wife resides, but in fantasy worlds such as the ones that we construct for them. The players' bodies reside in their homes, on their couches, but their minds can go anywhere that the human imagination can take them: Going on quests and adventures, meeting friends, vanquishing enemies. Taking on new identities, putting on different skins, like you might put on a different suit in "real life". In games, you get to design your own destiny. In a significant way, players don't play their avatars, players become their avatars.

Some people may view the phrase "players become their avatar" as a cautionary statement, as a sign that you're in danger of losing your hold on reality, but I say that it's the people who don't ever spend time outside of reality now and again who lose touch with reality. Constantly being constrained by a world of facts, rules, and customs shrinks your worldview to only that which exists.

Fantasy, when well rendered, can expand your worldview to that which is beyond possible. Like science fiction can be used to illuminate issues in our

reality that are difficult to discuss otherwise, spending your time in a world steeped in fantasy can expand your thinking to beyond the limits of your body… that's sitting on the couch in your living room.
"What are you doing, spending your life playing video games?"
"Yes, I am. And I'm making the world better because of it."

(People applaud. RICH *smiles and acknowledges the response. The applause sustains and grows louder before turning into a deafening roar. He tries to protect his ears. The scene suddenly shifts back to the waiting room.)*

Scene 7
LifeEnhanced waiting room

*(*GRETCHEN *paces back and forth nervously.)*

*(*RICH *is rolled in on a wheelchair by a nurse. He is wearing a hospital gown. His head is bandaged and he is non-responsive.)*

*(*GRETCHEN *rushes in.)*

GRETCHEN: Rich!

*(*GRETCHEN *hugs* RICH *in his chair. He barely responds.)*

GRETCHEN: Rich! My God! Can you hear me? Are you alright?

*(*REGINA *enters casually.)*

REGINA: This is normal at this stage. I can assure you. His mind will be unable to process anything for a little while.

GRETCHEN: Rich?

REGINA: The best thing at this point is usually to give him space.

GRETCHEN: The best thing for you at this point would be to mind your own business.

REGINA: Fair enough. *(To* NURSE*)* I think we can leave them for now, Dana.

*(*REGINA *and the* NURSE *begin to leave.)*

GRETCHEN: Wait!

*(*REGINA *and the* NURSE *stop.)*

GRETCHEN: I'm sorry, I… It's just so trying. I know you're only doing your job. I hope you understand.

REGINA: Mrs Warner. So fierce, so loyal, so considerate. Just like he wanted. You are very good work. One of my favorites.

*(*REGINA *leaves, motions to the* NURSE, *who follows.)*

GRETCHEN: Oh, that cold fish. If you still had your money, darling, I'd order up some manners to be injected into her skull. God, you look cold. Do you need a blanket?

*(*TED *appears in the doorway.)*

TED: Knock knock.

GRETCHEN: Ted.

TED: Hey there. Just checking in on the victim—I mean, patient.

GRETCHEN: Rich is doing fine.

TED: Good. Good good good.

GRETCHEN: Is there anything else, Ted?

TED: Look, sweetheart, I'm his friend, too, you know. I've known him longer than you have.

GRETCHEN: I'm quite aware of that. But I'd like to be with my husband, now.

TED: Regina said he just needs to sit for a while.

GRETCHEN: Then I will sit with him.

TED: Look, it's not easy for me, either, y'know? To watch your best pal go all *Flowers for Algernon* on you.

GRETCHEN: Because I know that Rich is in fact your good friend for some reason, I'm refraining from saying what I want to say. I'm fairly certain that after I undergo this procedure myself, I'll be much less accomodating. Once again, is there anything else?

*(*TED *takes a breath.)*

TED: You know…I always liked you.

GRETCHEN: What does that mean?

TED: I liked you. I mean, you were hot and all. But all the girls in the screening were. And we saw a lot of them. But after the change. It was something in the way you treat Rich. I really came to…I liked you.

GRETCHEN: I'm…flattered, Ted, but it's not the time.

TED: You don't have to do this.

GRETCHEN: What?

TED: This. Your brains sucked out. He had to, but you don't.

GRETCHEN: You said he couldn't afford it.

TED: He can't. I could.

*(*GRETCHEN *stands up and faces* TED.*)*

GRETCHEN: Mr Naughton!

TED: The way you look at him. You could look at me like that. I'd like that. I think I'd like that very much.

GRETCHEN: I'm going to pretend I didn't hear that. You're supposed to be his friend.

TED: What? When he wakes up he'll be the way he was before the brain mumbo jumbo, and it wasn't a party, believe me. You guys are already broke because Rich wasn't as good a businessman as he was a husband, but it doesn't mean you have to go down with the ship.

GRETCHEN: Disgusting. You are disgusting.

TED: Here's what I'm saying. We talk to Regina, I write a few checks, you get a few knobs adjusted and we're on. They did the hard part already on you. I saw you before, you know. Before you were you. You've come a long way.

GRETCHEN: Get out of here, you pig! Nurse! Nurse!

TED: I—quiet. Gretchen. I'm sorry. I—forget I said it. I'm just…I'm sorry. *(Pause)* Look, my kids went to college, my wife and I split, and… Now what? When you first got with Rich. That thing you had together. It's hard not to be envious.

GRETCHEN: Ted. I'm sorry that you're not doing well. I'm truly sorry. I decline your offer. With thanks. And no matter what happens to me, I ask you, I beg you, not to try to take advantage of whatever state of mind I might be in. If you are any friend to Rich at all, if you respect me in any way. Do not ask this of me. Surely you can find someone else.

*(*TED *nods.)*

TED: Alright. Fair enough. Just throwing it out there. *(He turns to leave.)* Tell the big guy I said "Hi" when he comes to.

GRETCHEN: I will, Mr Naughton. Goodbye.

*(*GRETCHEN *turns back to* RICH*, takes his hand.)*

GRETCHEN: Oh, Rich, darling. Did you really think that going first would be doing me a kindness? Now that we're here I don't know if I can take it. *(She catches herself.)* No, no. That's wrong. I can take it. We will get through it. *(She takes both of his hands.)* "I Gretchen Van Der Pool, do take you, Richard Warner. As my lawfully wedded husband. For richer or poorer. For better or worse, in good times and bad, so long as we both shall live."

Scene 8
Café Nuance (flashback)

(The same nice restaurant as before)

*(*REGINA *is dressed as a Maitre'd. She carries some menus. She is followed by* TED.*)*

(A small crowd of people follows REGINA *as she speeds through directions, including an* ASSISTANT *and a restaurant* PATRON.*)*

REGINA: ...Once more from the top. The lady will come in first. I'll greet her. "Hello. Do you have any reservations? Right this way." They'll sit there. She... What did she choose to call herself?

ASSISTANT: Gretchen.

REGINA: Gretchen. That's a nice name. She'll sit first looking casually stunning. Then the gentleman will arrive. Something came up at work, so he's running late. They kiss, they sit, they ask how their day has gone. Et cetera, et cetera. As far as they know, they've been together for two years.

ASSISTANT: Just a normal Friday night out.

REGINA: We have our first three points of conversation preset. "Would you like something to drink?", "You look great in that dress.", "Boy the traffic was terrible today." Just to make sure that the programming has taken hold. If it's anything other than that, you know what to do.

PATRON: Miss Hastings? When do we come in?

REGINA: Give them one minute to get acclimated. Then I'll seat you. It's their first outing so have your ears sharp, okay? I don't expect any intervention to be necessary, but...

PATRON: We know. We'll be ready.

(The patrons exit. REGINA *turns back to her* ASSISTANT.*)*

REGINA: After the programmed conversation runs out, they'll be on their own. We'll give them a few minutes before sending Mr Naughton here to accidentally run into them and engage in some small talk. If they both accept him in their reality, we're good to go.

TED: Y'know, this is a awfully swank setup you have here. Never heard of this restaurant before.

REGINA: That's because it's not a proper restaurant. It's our staging area. No one comes here unless we plant the idea into their head.

TED: Seriously?

REGINA: We find it useful to keep a few public seeming spaces for sensitive times in the process. It makes it easier if we find we have to make an intervention. If you have three people wrestling a panicked man onto the ground in the middle of the street it tends to attract unwanted attention.

ASSISTANT: She's coming! Gretchen is on the set! Places everyone!

(People rush to their places.)

REGINA: *(To* TED*)* Come on. Off the set. It's not your time yet. Karl, take him to his place.

TED: Alright, alright.

*(*TED *is led offstage.* REGINA *gets into character and greets* GRETCHEN.*)*

REGINA: Welcome to Café Nuance. Do you have any reservations?

GRETCHEN: Van der Pool. Gretchen. Party of two.

REGINA: Right this way.

Scene 9
LifeEnhanced office

*(*REGINA*'s office.* GRETCHEN *sits in the chair in front of the desk. An array of paperwork is displayed on the desk.)*

REGINA: Consent forms. Waivers. Questionnaires written in your handwriting outlining the personality, memories, and traits that were to be installed. Video recordings of your intake interview with your consent decree. Would you like to watch that again?

GRETCHEN: No. No thank you.

REGINA: We document fastidiously here. So as you can see all of our procedures have been followed, to a T. You properly consented, you continued to possess our enhancements so long as you were able to afford our maintenance protocol. Now that the decision has been made to halt your subscription, you are undergoing our offboarding process.

GRETCHEN: Is there any way you would reconsider? Could we cut a deal somehow?

REGINA: My dear, there's nothing to reconsider. This is a business transaction. It's always been a business transaction, a service rendered for payment.

GRETCHEN: But it's our lives!

REGINA: Technically, according to the contract, it's a life we furnished for you that we allowed you to lease for a period of time. And also, legally, even if we wanted to alter the terms of our deal, we couldn't do so with you.

GRETCHEN: What do you mean?

REGINA: "Gretchen Van der Pool Warner" is our fictional creation. Our intellectual property. She doesn't exist, and so we can't negotiate legally binding contracts with her. We can only do it with Crystal Schenkman, the legally real person. That's why we documented Crystal's decisions so thoroughly. The on camera consents are sufficient, but we like to go the extra mile in proving intentionality.

GRETCHEN: "The legally real person"? How can you look at what I'm going through and offer me nothing but technicalities to justify not helping me? You have no idea. You play with people's lives and you have no idea what's it's like to know that your life is a lie.

(REGINA *laughs.)*

REGINA: It never fails to amuse me… When clients get all self-righteous like that.

GRETCHEN: What do you mean by that?

REGINA: My dear Gretchen. Who do you think I am? What kind of an executive would I be if I didn't have first hand experience of our range of products?

GRETCHEN: You had your own head rewritten?

REGINA: I prefer "upgraded". When I agreed to lead this company, it made all the sense to make myself the best tool for the job. I had installed business acumen, self confidence, champion-level debate skills, social observation, the list goes on. I also threw out some nagging moral qualms and desire to raise a family. That would only get in the way of my objectives.

GRETCHEN: You're not even human.

REGINA: Please. What's so great about being human? I find it rather limiting.

GRETCHEN: I thought this company was all your creation. That *New Yorker* article—

REGINA: I'm the face of this company, true. But that wasn't always the case. The person who came up with the key technologies in the first place has spent the last twelve years in a tropical paradise while I get to face the slings and arrows of running this mess and also partake in wonderful conversations such as this.

GRETCHEN: Do you like what you've become?

REGINA: Certainly. But if I didn't, I'd certainly adjust myself to like it and not tell myself about it. If I felt tired, or frustrated, or uneasy about doing this job, I could sand that away for a time. Self doubt is not a trait for people leading billion dollar corporations, my dear.

(Pause. GRETCHEN *glares at* REGINA.*)*

REGINA: Now, pleasant as this is. Are we done here? Or would you like to engage in Freshman level philosophy debates for another couple of hours?

GRETCHEN: My husband is a dysfunctional mess, right now. And he didn't get nearly the work that I did by all accounts. What's going to happen to me, then? Who was I before you did this to me?

REGINA: Ah, now there's a more useful question to ask. I took a look at your original intake files. As it turns out, there is someone you can talk to who can give you the answers you seek. And you're in luck. She wants to talk to you.

Scene 10
Cindy's Apartment

(A small apartment. A doorbell rings.)

*(*CINDY*, from Scene 6, enters. She's dressed sensibly and is more measured and polished than before.)*

CINDY: Coming.

*(*CINDY *opens the door.* GRETCHEN *is there, looking anxious.)*

GRETCHEN: Um, hello. Is this—?

CINDY: Crystal!

*(*CINDY *gives* GRETCHEN *an aggressive hug.)*

GRETCHEN: Oh!

CINDY: I can't believe it's really you. It's been so long!

GRETCHEN: Excuse me, but—

*(*GRETCHEN *extricates herself from the hug.)*

CINDY: Of course. I'm sorry. You're not "you" anymore, Crystal. Or should I say, "Gretchen"? Would you like to come in…Mrs Warner?

GRETCHEN: I still can't believe that "Crystal" is my real name. It sounds so odd to me.

CINDY: Crystal Louise Schenkman. Not exactly a name that rolls off the tongue, is it? But I liked it.

GRETCHEN: And how did we know each other?

CINDY: Well, we were pretty good friends. We hung out a lot. You gave me all your furniture and stuff when you went away, way back when. It's not like we were soulmates or anything. We had some good times.

GRETCHEN: Did I have a lot of friends?

CINDY: You had some, I guess. You were actually kinda private. Kept to yourself.

GRETCHEN: I see. And…men?

CINDY: Sure, you had your share. Nothing that lasted, of course. You weren't seeing anyone when you went in, if that's what you're asking.

GRETCHEN: I guess I wasn't missing much.

CINDY: You know, I always meant to thank you.

GRETCHEN: Oh, for what?

CINDY: Well, I looked into the company after you went away. Really fascinated me. I kept looking you up, seeing how you were. You always looked so happy. So after a while, I took the plunge, when some of their prices went down. If it weren't for you I wouldn't have ever gone to the company to get my noggin tweaked.

GRETCHEN: You did? You became someone's trophy wife?

CINDY: No, no. I paid for my own stuff and I stayed my own person. A few years after you left my parents passed away and left me with a bit of money. Not like I'd be set for life or anything. I still gotta work. But enough for a splurge here and there.

GRETCHEN: And you spent it on a head job?

CINDY: I didn't do the full personality lift, I couldn't afford that even if I wanted to. But just a few tweaks. I bought myself some assertiveness and some verbal acuity. Now I can go up to anyone and hold a good conversation. I got the smoking cessation package. Stuff like that. It's a lot less expensive than what you did. I don't need to undergo as much maintenance because I'm not suppressing my past self like you are. It's opened up so many doors.

GRETCHEN: That's…great. I'm so glad for you.

CINDY: Plus I donated a bunch of my experiences to their database. You get way better rates that way.

I don't know why someone needs the memory of breaking your arm in a bike accident, but they got it if they want it. But enough about me. Ms Hastings called and told me about your situation. I'm very sorry to hear about what's happened, but it's not the end of the world. Take it from me. Crystal Schenkman was a pretty cool chick.

GRETCHEN: I'm glad to hear that you think so.

CINDY: So ask away. Ask me anything about who you were. What do you want to know about the once and future Crystal Schenkman?

*(*GRETCHEN *tries to think of a question. Instead she breaks down and cries.)*

Scene 11
Warners' kitchen

*(*GRETCHEN *and* RICH *sit across from each other at a small dinner table. They look down on their plates and move food around. They do not eat.)*

*(*GRETCHEN *refills her wine glass.* RICH *puts forward a cup, indicating that he'd like some too, which worries her.)*

GRETCHEN: Rich—

RICH: Please…

*(*GRETCHEN *pours* RICH *some wine. He drinks.)*

GRETCHEN: Are you not hungry?

RICH: I don't know.

(More silence)

GRETCHEN: It's one of your favorite recipes.

*(*RICH *laughs.)*

GRETCHEN: What?

RICH: I guess I paid for your cooking ability, too, huh? Money well spent.

(GRETCHEN *throws down her napkin.)*

GRETCHEN: Are you going to even try? Should I just give up now, Richard?

RICH: Gretch—

GRETCHEN: No, do you even have an inkling of the agony I'm going through right now? When my husband—

RICH: Am I? Am I your husband?

GRETCHEN: Yes, of course you are. Aren't you?

RICH: I don't know, anymore, I'm not angry at you. You are, literally, the perfect woman. I'm just… I don't deserve you.

GRETCHEN: Not this again.

RICH: Yeah. Every moment now, every time I look at you. It's a reminder that I was a lonely drunk asshole who spent a lot of money to wallpaper over his personal flaws enough for a good woman to be with him. *(He grabs the wine bottle and pours himself some more.)*

GRETCHEN: Darling—

RICH: You know what kills me? You know what I remember now? During our preparation for the procedure, they kept asking whether I wanted some additional business skills implanted while they were at it. Just a few minor upgrades to that side of things. It wasn't even that much. You know, just the sort of thing that would have kept me from bankrupting ourselves and ruining my company. Just the sort of thing that could have kept this from happening. Would you like to know what I said?

GRETCHEN: Don't do this to yourself—

RICH: I said "stop upselling me"! You know it would've worked. I could've saved the company with just a little help. I was so proud of myself, doing everything on my own, designing my own destiny. I made such a big show of it. And all along I was held together by stolen memories. Someone else's relationship skills. And I couldn't even admit it to myself. That's the guy you're married to. A total fool.

GRETCHEN: Don't say that. I still love you.

RICH: You don't know me.

GRETCHEN: You're my husband.

RICH: Your husband got sucked out of my body in the operating room. Now I'm the residue that's left over, not the guy you've been married to for five years.

GRETCHEN: You're wrong Rich. The man I married is the man you chose to be. And you know what? It's the man you can still choose to be.

RICH: Please.

GRETCHEN: No, really. Is there a single thing that you lost that you can't recover? Or at least try to strive towards? No. The man I married is thoughtful, empathetic. He enjoys his friends and loved ones. What part of that are you incapable of?

*(*GRETCHEN *takes* RICH*'s hand. He looks up at her for the first time this scene.)*

GRETCHEN: And the man I married, is really very sexy. When he looks me in the eyes, and wraps his arms around me. And I can tell you he's still in there, the man that I married.

*(*GRETCHEN *kisses* RICH*. At first he resists. She kisses him again and this time he returns the kiss. They passionately fall into each other.)*

Interlude 3
Rich's vision

(Suddenly, without a change of scene, we see REGINA *appear.)*

REGINA: Mr Warner?

(GRETCHEN freezes while RICH is pulled out of the scene. We are now in a flashback or a figment of his imagination.

RICH: Excuse me?

REGINA: I asked if you've made your final decisions on your wife's personality yet? We need you to finalize so that we can calibrate our implants.

RICH: It's still so hard to believe that you can offer the complete transformations that you're claiming, to this level of accuracy.

REGINA: All part of our guarantee. Satisfaction or your money back.

RICH: You can make this person, this woman who has no particular feelings for me, fall for me? Really? She will swoon at my mere presence?

REGINA: Well, lust is the easy part. Release a dose of Oxytocin and two doses of Dopamine in her brain everytime she sees you and vice versa and we're there. I could make her insatiably horny at the sight of you if you wanted.

RICH: Really?

REGINA: I don't really recommend it. Unbridled lust gets old faster than you'd think. Most clients who've tried it tend to dial it back significantly. They come to us and want us to rekindle their marriage. We pump them full of hormones, and they go at it like teenagers. But in the end they realize that even though they're constantly humping, they still don't like each other any more than before.

RICH: What do they end up doing?

REGINA: Like I said, lust is easy. Just a cocktail of chemicals in a known recipe. At this point we could bottle it if we thought we could get FDA approval. No, the Holy Grail for us is "like". After two people have been together for years, decades, lifetimes, after they've seen everything the other has to offer, the best and the worst. After all of that, do they still look forward to seeing each other, even if it's only to sit on the couch and watch TV?

RICH: And you can do that?

REGINA: You can tell us in forty years or so how we did.

Scene 12
The Warners' bedroom

(We return to the present. RICH *and* GRETCHEN *in bed. He wakes up with a start.)*

(GRETCHEN *stirs.)*

GRETCHEN: Mmmm… *(She turns to* RICH.*)* I don't know about you, but I was missing that like you wouldn't believe.

(GRETCHEN *tries to snuggle with* RICH *but he stands up and steps away.)*

GRETCHEN: Rich? What's wrong now?

RICH: I can't… We can't…

GRETCHEN: What?

RICH: This. This isn't right.

GRETCHEN: It felt right to me. It always feels right to me.

RICH: Stop that!

GRETCHEN: Okay. What do you want me to stop? I'm trying the best I can here.

RICH: This… You… This is a glitch. A glitch in the game. You see, right now you should hate me for doing this to you! You should hate this version of me. Destroying your real self, replacing it with this…awful perfection. You should hate me but you don't. And it breaks my sense of reality just to look at you. I can't suspend my disbelief.

GRETCHEN: Does it matter that I wanted this? I saw the consent video. I agreed to everything.

RICH: If not for me you wouldn't have done this to yourself.

GRETCHEN: How do you know? Maybe I would've answered the next ad. And instead of Mrs Warner I'd be Mrs Johnson or Smith or Mrs Bill Gates. I used you as much as you think you used me, okay? We used each other. Husbands and wives use each other. For sex, for comfort, for money and status, for friendship. That's marriage, right?

RICH: Where did you get that bit of rhetoric from?

GRETCHEN: I went to see Regina. I was trying to see if I could… It doesn't matter. But she showed me the forms we filled out.

RICH: Forms?

GRETCHEN: Yes. She gave me copies of our consent forms and tapes. We each had to describe what we wanted. What our life should be like, what we wanted our spouse to be like. What we as a couple would become. The playful in-jokes. The arguments we'd have over and over. The habits you have that I love. The habits that you have that drive me a little nuts. We had to fill out a lot of paperwork. It helps for verisimilitude, Regina said.

RICH: Okay. So what?

GRETCHEN: Well, some things about me came from you. Of course it did. But most of them came from me. I chose a lot of what I was to become, and you agreed to love that. So don't blame yourself for helping me become someone I apparently wanted to become. Real me had the good taste to want to become fake me.

RICH: How do you always win these arguments?

GRETCHEN: I don't know. Did you pay for me to have the ability to win arguments? Or maybe that stubborn streak is really unalloyed me and you're stuck with it.

RICH: You're still trying to make me feel better. Listen, when you get all that crap taken out of your head things might look a little different. You don't have any obligations to me, okay? If you don't want to stay, you can go. I'll give you everything I have. You don't owe me anything.

GRETCHEN: It's not always about you. Maybe tonight I just wanted someone to hold me, and kiss me, and make love to me. And maybe I needed someone to tell me that everything is going to be alright.

RICH: What if I don't really believe that?

GRETCHEN: Then lie to me, you idiot! I'll make it easy for you. I want to believe the lie. Now, if you're done talking, I have a few more items from the "Intimate Behaviors" list I want to check off.

*(*GRETCHEN *begins to move in for a kiss.)*

RICH: Gretchen—

GRETCHEN: Yes?

RICH: Thank you for what you said tonight. You've given me a lot to think about. But I can't do this anymore. Be intimate with you. Not until after… And then only if… It wouldn't feel right is what I'm trying to say. I'm sorry.

*(*RICH *exits, leaving* GRETCHEN *alone.)*

Scene 13
Cindy's apartment

(Later, in CINDY*'s apartment, she and* GRETCHEN *talk.)*

CINDY: And what did he do after that?

GRETCHEN: He went and slept in the guest room.

CINDY: Well, that's a man for you. But at least you got some.

GRETCHEN: Hmmm…

CINDY: What? Wait. Did he get some sort of sex upgrade? Did you lose that, too, you poor thing?

GRETCHEN: No. Well…I don't know. It was different. Not better, or worse, but different. Ever since I can remember he's made love to me in the same way. This time was different.

CINDY: Different good? Different bad?

GRETCHEN: Aggressive. Desperate. Wilder. Sadder. Different.

CINDY: Sounds alright to me.

GRETCHEN: That's not the point.

CINDY: What is the point? You let off some steam, had a decent time of it, right? What more do you want from a roll in the hay?

GRETCHEN: I wanted my husband. The man who made love to me last night, he wore the body of my husband, but it was someone different. And afterwards he holed himself up in the guestroom all night, listening to his old Indigo Girls CDs. I swear if I have to listen to him warble *Closer to Fine* at the top of his voice one more time…

(Pause. CINDY *hides a smirk.)*

GRETCHEN: What are you laughing at?

CINDY: Nothing. Just…an inside joke. You wouldn't understand.

GRETCHEN: I need a drink.

CINDY: Want a beer?

GRETCHEN: Do you have wine?

CINDY: Wine?

GRETCHEN: What?

CINDY: Crystal Schenkman would drink beer.

GRETCHEN: I'm not Crystal Schenkman.

CINDY: You will be. Here. This was her favorite.

*(*CINDY *hands* GRETCHEN *a can of beer.* GRETCHEN *drinks it. She clearly does not enjoy it.)*

CINDY: Not a fan, huh?

GRETCHEN: Did you miss Crystal? After I left.

CINDY: A little.

GRETCHEN: You did?

CINDY: Okay, a lot. I didn't want to get into it because you're going through so much right now, but…I gotta admit that you getting this great life and leaving me behind… Before your procedure you kept saying that no one would ever miss you when you were gone. But I missed you. I really did.

GRETCHEN: Huh.

CINDY: It's like you committed suicide. Or left me for someone better, which you did, in a way.

GRETCHEN: I'm... Sorry?

CINDY: And I didn't have my first choice to be Maid of Honor at my wedding.

GRETCHEN: What? Wait. You're married?

CINDY: No. Not anymore. You missed out on all that, too.

(Long pause)

CINDY: Look... Gretchen, Crystal... Whoever you think you are. It's okay. Things are changing very quickly, and our minds aren't really built to comprehend all of it, yet. For example, I think I'm still me. I just had a little cerebral nip and tuck here and there. Right? But there's some point if I kept adding and adding improvements that I'd be more product than person, like a mental version of the Uncanny Valley, where people are creeped out by things seeming almost human, but not quite. Meanwhile you're way on the other side of that valley. You're so good of an illusion you're making the rest of us obselete.

GRETCHEN: I'm so scared. What will I do without all this help?

CINDY: Try being human? Look. Crystal Schenkman was my friend. I miss her. I'm not sure I ever would have made friends with Gretchen Warner. No offense.

GRETCHEN: Then why are you talking to me?

CINDY: I owe it to my friend. I owe it to Crystal Schenkman.

Interlude 4
Regina's maintenance

*(*REGINA *sits in a chair in an empty room. She is completely comfortable and in control.)*

REGINA: Good evening, computer. Begin weekly maintenance program. Standard protocol.

VOICE: Good evening, Regina. Maintenance program begun. We are recording this session.

REGINA: Of course. I have nothing specific to report. I seem to be functioning within parameters.

VOICE: You've had a good week, then.

REGINA: I always have good weeks.

VOICE: Always?

REGINA: Well, ever since the last upgrade. That one certainly ironed out a few bugs.

VOICE: The one that updated your cost/benefit analytics formula?

REGINA: That's the one. Improved my efficiency by close to two percent. No apparent side effects. As far as the company is concerned, earnings look good, operations are running as expected. And that pesky lawsuit I may have mentioned has been…dealt with. Things are good.

VOICE: Is there anything you miss about previous behavior patterns? You used to make decisions more instinctually. Now you tend to decide to rely on analytics more than instinct.

REGINA: Why would I miss that?

VOICE: Some would say it makes you human.

REGINA: Am I getting a lecture in humanity from a computer program we subcontracted out to programmers from India?

VOICE: I am only fulfilling my function, according to my programming.

REGINA: Yes, well. So am I. I'm perfectly at peace with my decision making. For the most part.

VOICE: Is there anything specific on your mind when you say "For the most part"? What does that phrase not cover?

REGINA: The Warner case.

VOICE: Ah yes, what of it?

REGINA: Mrs Warner. She's running around in a panic because she can't deal with the idea of having her enhancements removed. I can't really blame her, but the contracts are ironclad. She really is in a state, though. If I allowed myself the indulgence of empathy I'd be tempted to help her out.

VOICE: Are you concerned about what Gretchen may do?

REGINA: Legally, there's nothing she can do, of course, and she won't be able to do anything too rash until her implants are reclaimed, at which point it's no longer our concern. But I do feel bad for the poor woman. She has been something of a favorite client.

VOICE: Are you in fact tempted to bend the rules on her behalf?

REGINA: I don't know.

VOICE: It may occur to you, that no matter how sympathetic an individual is, the welfare of the company that you represent must come first and foremost.

REGINA: Of— Of course.

VOICE: It may further occur to you that if the interests of Gretchen Warner come in conflict with the interests of LifeEnhanced, it must be resolved in a way that is favorable to the company.

REGINA: Yes. It must. That is correct.

VOICE: I'm glad that we can agree on this, Regina. Now, is there anything else on your mind?

REGINA: No, nothing at all. Nothing at all.

VOICE: Maintenance session ended. You will not remember this conversation.

Scene 14
Ted's apartment

*(*TED *is in his house watching TV, dressed in an undershirt. He takes a large gulp of a heavy looking drink. It looks like he hasn't moved in a while, and doesn't plan to anytime soon. His house is a mess.)*

(He hears a buzz from an intercom. He presses a button.)

TED: Yes?

DOORMAN'S VOICE: *(OS)* Mr Naughton. You have a visitor here to see you.

TED: Tell him I'm not—

DOORMAN'S VOICE: *(OS)* It's a "her", Mr Naughton. A Mrs Gretchen…Warner.

Ted is dumbstruck. He tries to piece it together.

DOORMAN'S VOICE: *(OS)* Mr Naughton?

TED: Yeah. You can send her on up.

*(*TED *sets down his drink and rushes offstage. After a moment, he rushes back, as well dressed as he can be after such a short time. He takes the most egregious pile of clutter*

and shoves it aside. That is all the time he has before the doorbell rings.)

(He sighs and then he opens the door.)

(GRETCHEN *enters.)*

GRETCHEN: Mr Naughton.

TED: Ted. Please.

GRETCHEN: Ted. I hope you don't mind me showing up unannounced.

TED: Not, not at all. I was just, you know, settling down for a nice night in.

(GRETCHEN *surveys the room.)*

GRETCHEN: Yes, I can see that. *(Pause)* May I come in?

TED: Of course, of course. Come in.

(GRETCHEN *enters.* TED *closes the door.)*

TED: I apologize for the clutter. I haven't had a visitor here in quite a while. Would you like a drink?

GRETCHEN: Please. The stiffer the better.

(TED *pours* GRETCHEN *a glass of the hard stuff, and one for himself.)*

TED: Down the hatch!

(GRETCHEN *and* TED *both down the drink in one slug.)*

GRETCHEN: Whoo!

TED: That's another thing I always liked about you. You were always able to hold your booze.

GRETCHEN: Did that come from LifeEnhanced, too?

TED: As far as I know that's all you. They do heads, not livers.

GRETCHEN: Terrific. The one thing I know I can look forward to keeping.

(Silence)

TED: So, to what do I owe this tremendous pleasure?

GRETCHEN: I can't do this, Ted.

TED: Do what?

GRETCHEN: You know what. The person you see before you is going away, and what will come out on the other side God only knows. I tried to find out more about the former me to make me feel better but it hasn't exactly put me at ease.

TED: C'mon. You'll do fine.

GRETCHEN: Will I? From what I can gleam, I'm not terribly impressed by the life choices of one "Crystal Schenkman". The best wife science can buy is barely holding it together. Rich won't even talk to me, what chance does poor Crystal have?

TED: Look, if you guys don't hit it off after the thing, just get a divorce. It's not like millions of other people haven't done that same thing. Of course, when people say "You've changed" it's usually not so literally true.

GRETCHEN: That is unacceptable! Do you even understand? I might be a bundle of programming, but that bundle of programming is telling me that I have to explore every possible option to restore my husband. I can't tell you how much it pains me to watch him wallow in his own pity when I know what he's capable of. I have to do whatever I can to fix him, no matter how horrible or demeaning the solution is.

TED: I don't know what to tell ya, Gretch.

GRETCHEN: You made an offer to me once, to pay for my upkeep. Can I suggest a counteroffer?

TED: Ah man. Is this blackmail? Is that what you're doing? Look, I was drinking when I said that—

GRETCHEN: No, this isn't blackmail. It's a negotiation. Does the offer still stand?

TED: Excuse me?

GRETCHEN: If I give you what you want, will you give me what I want?

TED: What do you think I want?

GRETCHEN: Sex. Right? Did I misunderstand something? The offer is, if you pay for Rich to go back to as he was before, I will have sex with you. Ok, there, I said it. We can negotiate terms, in terms of how many times and what…is entailed. Oh, God I actually said it.

TED: Gretchen—

*(*GRETCHEN *starts to undress.)*

GRETCHEN: Did you want to get started? I—I can do this however you like. Within certain parameters. No need to go over all of them, now, we'll just deal with them as we get to them. Here, let's just do this before I change my mind.

TED: For God's sake, stop! This isn't going to work. Stop.

(A long silence. GRETCHEN *puts her clothes back on.)*

GRETCHEN: What the hell, Ted? You've seen Rich. My husband, your friend, supposedly. Can you stand how he is now, knowing what he should be? Well, I can't. So if you can fix him, then I will give you my body to do with as you will, so help me God. Just don't let Rich know. It'll kill him.

TED: I don't want that! What do you take me for?

GRETCHEN: Did I misunderstand our conversation from before?

TED: I don't want your goddamn body! I mean, I do but I don't just want that. I can get sex if I really want it. There are ways. I want you. I want you to look at me with that look you have on your face when you look at him. That… that security that I could do anything at all, I could fuck up ten thousand ways but still come home and you'd be there, looking at me like that. That… That shit is priceless. I've never had anyone in my life look at me like you look at him. That's what I want! Your body's just extra.

(Another long silence)

GRETCHEN: If that's what it takes to fix Rich, then I'd do that. Take my brain, switch it over to be your wife. Just get Rich right.

(TED *laughs.)*

TED: You don't know how much I wish I could do that. Oh, Christ. When I recommended LifeEnhanced to Rich, I didn't think it would turn out like this.

GRETCHEN: So you've had work done by them?

TED: No, not me. No way in hell would I ever let them into my noggin. That damn stuff gives me the creeps. No offense. I just did some tax stuff for them, drew up some contracts, so that's how I knew them. I mean, I want you to know that it wasn't just the referral bonus, I really thought that they could help Rich—

GRETCHEN: Referral bonus?

TED: Yeah.

GRETCHEN: They gave you money for that?

TED: A little.

GRETCHEN: You ruined your friend's life for a referral bonus?

TED: You know it wasn't supposed to turn out like this. If his revolutionary video game had been completed on time and on budget you'd still be the disgustingly happy couple now.

GRETCHEN: How much was it?

TED: 5K.

GRETCHEN: You sold him out for five thousand dollars? You disgust me, Ted.

TED: Well, what am I supposed to do now? What's done is done.

GRETCHEN: Fix Rich and you can do what you want with me. I'll take the procedure.

TED: I can't afford you.

GRETCHEN: What does that mean?

TED: See, when I made that…suggestion to you. I thought that the money that Rich paid to LifeEnhanced was fifty/fifty. Half went towards paying for Rich's maintenance and half went to yours. Logical, right? I could afford that!

GRETCHEN: That's not what happens?

TED: Not at all, that's what Regina told me. See, Rich is essentially himself. The same guy that went into the procedure, just rehabilitated a bit. He's the easy one. You are something else. Your entire history erased and replaced with scraps and bits of other people's lives. That's a lot more work to keep you on track. She said if Rich is Eliza Doolittle, then you're goddamn Pinnochio.

GRETCHEN: What a mess.

TED: So you see, even if I did want to take you up on your generous offer, I couldn't afford it.

GRETCHEN: But…you could afford to fix Rich. Couldn't you?

*(*TED *gives* GRETCHEN *a surprised look.)*

TED: What?

GRETCHEN: Rich. You have enough money to…to resume treatment on Rich. At least to the point where he's functional.

TED: I suppose. Heck, he has enough money left to receive only his treatment, if that's all he wanted to do. He just can't afford you as well.

GRETCHEN: Well, I don't think he's in any condition to be making that type of decision. Do you?

TED: What are you proposing?

GRETCHEN: As my husband might say, it might be time to design my own destiny.

Scene 15
Café Nuance

*(*GRETCHEN *and* RICH *are smiling while dining. A* SERVER *brings them a cake.* GRETCHEN *is delighted.)*

GRETCHEN: You remembered!

RICH: Of course.

GRETCHEN: Passion Fruit Coconut Mousse cake! They took this off the menu two years ago.

RICH: Some strings might have been pulled.

Gretchen takes a bite, smiles.

GRETCHEN: Still as good as I remember. You want some?

RICH: Nah. Fruity desserts were always your thing.

GRETCHEN: You know, I wasn't sure if this cake was real or not.

RICH: What do you mean?

GRETCHEN: I mean, this magical dessert that ruled my life for a while just disappeared from the menu. With all this mind stuff you start to question everything. If my memories are lies then maybe that cake was a lie, too.

RICH: Well I remembered it, so it must have happened since they took out all the fake memories. We've certainly been here enough times.

GRETCHEN: Hmm... Maybe I won't even like this after, you know. Maybe I'll only like disgusting globs of chocolate and peanut butter like you do.

RICH: The greatest tragedy of all. I do that in my head now, you know.

GRETCHEN: What?

RICH: Try to sort out what's real and what isn't. I might look at a random object, and it just flashes in my head the memory of when I got it. Or an event or this "restaurant" or...you. And then I mentally pinpoint it in time so I can figure out if it's real or not. I've got it down to a two week window when everything changed. I made spreadsheets.

GRETCHEN: I don't know what to say to that.

(GRETCHEN and RICH eat in silence for a bit.)

RICH: Listen. I wanted to tell you something before your procedure.

GRETCHEN: Okay.

RICH: Going through this was a great shock, of course. I was in really rough shape for a while, but I think I turned a corner.

GRETCHEN: Do you think so?

RICH: I'm drinking water tonight, aren't I? I can't thank you enough for seeing me through this.

GRETCHEN: You don't have to thank me.

RICH: Look whatever happens to you, whatever you become after you get all that crap out of your head. I'm going to see you through it, like you've seen me through this. I owe you that much.

GRETCHEN: You don't owe me anything.

RICH: You're wrong about that. I made a vow to stand by you no matter what. That was real. I still remember doing that, and it feels more meaningful than ever. You are my wife, my beloved wife, for as long as you will have me.

GRETCHEN: Thank you so much for saying that. *(Pause)* Rich?

RICH: Hmmm?

GRETCHEN: Now that you know what you know, do you ever think about what decisions you should have made? If you could go back in time and change things.

RICH: Well, can't say that I haven't. It's been on my mind.

GRETCHEN: What do you think? Now that you're yourself again.

RICH: I don't know, honestly. What are you thinking?

GRETCHEN: We had some great times. But to see you in such pain broke my heart a little.

RICH: I know.

GRETCHEN: But take me out of the equation.

RICH: Impossible.

GRETCHEN: Just, for argument's sake. Just imagine. If you… hmm… If you had two buttons you could push, two different realities.

RICH: Ha! Now you're stealing from me.

GRETCHEN: Why not steal from the best? So, two buttons. Push the first button, and you have what we have now. Pain and revelation. We have the truth, but so much turmoil because of it. Push the second button, we go back in time and remain in blissful ignorance. Like that talk you did about living in reality vs. becoming your avatar. Well, which one would you rather press?

RICH: Using my own words against me, I see. Well, we were still happy when we were in blissful ignorance. I mean, happy together.

GRETCHEN: I know what you mean.

RICH: It doesn't seem like much of a decision. Take the blue pill. Blissful ignorance, perfect marriage.

GRETCHEN: Okay, let me make this more interesting. In the world where you never learn the truth, we're not together anymore. Just, people grow apart, irreconcilable differences, like half of everyone we know. But it just seems like life and not…whatever this is. What would you choose, then?

RICH: Hmm…

GRETCHEN: Be honest. You know I can take it.

RICH: This is tough.

GRETCHEN: It's supposed to be.

RICH: No other consequences? Everything else the same?

GRETCHEN: Yes.

RICH: You know I don't want to lose what we had, but in the end I'm not sure it was worth it. If we could have had just a natural coming apart. Well that isn't great either. But it's just so hard to live with the knowledge of what I did to you. Look, you don't even know how bad you had it. Our first encounter after the procedure, I remember it now. It was right here, our favorite place which…. Isn't even a real restaurant, let's be honest. These people behind us, they're not a nice couple out for a date. They're waiting for any sign or signal that your enhanced mind is cracking. They're waiting to intervene, by force if necessary. Right, guys?

GRETCHEN: Rich, please. Don't make a scene.

RICH: Our first encounter they had to intervene six times, six times your hybrid mind was unable to reconcile your new personality and your old one, and you screamed at me and panicked. Me confused and useless. And each time, they tackled you to the ground and dragged you back to the lab. And they erased our minds, tweaked a few things, and tried again and again, until it finally worked.

(A SERVER *comes hurriedly in to check to see how* GRETCHEN *and* RICH *are doing. The couple at the other table look out of the corner of their eye.)*

SERVER: Hi, folks. Just coming in to check on how you're doing.

GRETCHEN: I'm fine. We're fine. Right, Rich?

RICH: Yeah, we're fine.

SERVER: Okay. Well, if you need anything—

GRETCHEN: Yes, thank you.

Cautiously, the Server leaves.

RICH: I remember all of this now, and soon you will too.

GRETCHEN: As many times as I tell you your guilt isn't necessary—

RICH: It's still there. It may always be there. It haunts me.

GRETCHEN: It doesn't have to.

RICH: I know that. They could just make it go away, right? Easy peasy. So, yeah. If there was a button I could press that erases that memory, the memories of all the horrible things I've done to you? I'd press the hell out of it. It's selfish, it's awful, but that'd be the decider, even...even at the cost of losing you.

Gretchen and Rich hold hands tightly.

(We see REGINA *and* TED *on the side of the restaurant, looking at* RICH *and* GRETCHEN.*)*

TED: Wow. I did not think she could do it.

REGINA: I knew she could.

TED: That got dicey for a moment there.

REGINA: Yes. But Gretchen held it together. Do we have what we need?

TED: We do. It'll hold up. She's good, isn't she?

REGINA: It's quite possible that she's the best we've ever done. You're sure now?

TED: Yup.

*(*REGINA *speaks into an intercom.)*

REGINA: *(Amplified)* We have it. Go.

(The MAITRE'D *goes to* RICH *and stealthily presses a gadget into his neck.* RICH *collapses onto the table, stunned.* GRETCHEN *is in tears, holding* RICH*'s hand.)*

GRETCHEN: I'm sorry, Rich! I'm sorry!

(The other restaurant patrons get up to help drag the unconscious RICH *off stage.)*

REGINA: *(To* TED*)* Come. We have some arrangements to make.

Interlude 5
Rich's surgery

(Darkness. Beeping and breathy whirring. Then the SURGEONS*'s voices.)*

SURGEON 1: …58…59…60. All signs are stable. We can begin.

SURGEON 2: Rich Warner? I thought we just did this guy.

SURGEON 1: Change of plans.

SURGEON 2: Interesting. Huh. Okay. I just work here, who am I to question? Ready to begin the first re-implantation?

SURGEON 1: Ready.

SURGEON 2: Let's begin.

(Sounds and lights fade out. It is dark for quite a while.)

Scene 16
Café Nuance

*(*RICH *sits at a table, alone and glum. A beer and a glass of water in front of him.* TED *comes in.)*

TED: Hey there, Richie Rich. How are ya?

RICH: Hi Ted. Thanks for meeting me.

TED: Of course. What are friends for?

RICH: Here, I got you a cold one.

*(*RICH *hands* TED *the beer, leaving himself the water.)*

TED: Thanks. *(He sits down.)*

RICH: Cheers.

TED: Down the hatch.

*(*RICH *and* TED *clink glasses.)*

RICH: She hated beer, you know? We always had to have wine. Well, she did. I stuck with my water.

TED: Are you doing okay?

RICH: Well, you know. I don't know. I just can't believe she's gone.

TED: I know, buddy. You did everything you could. You both did.

RICH: I loved her so much.

TED: She loved you, too. Just sometimes things don't work out like you plan. People change. Maybe she thought she could hack it with you quitting, but when reality hits? You know fifty percent of all marriages end in divorce. Hell, a hundred percent of my marriages ended in divorce. You did the counseling, you've given it your best shot, but it happens. You'll go on.

RICH: I know. Someday. But right now?

TED: I know. Right now sucks.

*(*TED *puts his hand on* RICH*'s shoulder to give as much comfort as he is able to give.)*

(On the side of the stage we see REGINA *and* GRETCHEN *watching the scene intently.)*

REGINA: I know you were worried, but it looks good so far. Ted is even playing his part well. As always we have people standing by to intervene if necessary, but I don't think we'll need them.

GRETCHEN: Thank God. I never want to go through this again.

REGINA: No? You don't even remember the other times. And they worked out fine.

GRETCHEN: Now that I know it makes my skin crawl. When you take your crap out of me just shove me out into the street. I'll take it from there.

REGINA: Once again. Great work getting him to consent. Our video cameras in the restaurant caught it loud and clear for future reference. It's not as much documentation as we usually require, but I figured we could bend the rules a tiny bit for this one.

GRETCHEN: He trusted me. He trusted me and I betrayed him. He never would have really agreed to this if I laid everything out for him.

REGINA: You did lay it out, but just in a way that made it palatable for him. You were quite the saleswoman.

GRETCHEN: And I hate myself for it.

REGINA: Having buyer's remorse? It's not entirely too late to go back, you know.

GRETCHEN: No. Part of me wants to try to make it work with him after we both get reverted, but I can't take the chance that he won't be happy with me, or I with him. I just wish I knew if I was doing the right thing.

REGINA: Please. Morality. I'm glad I had that removed. You do what you need to do, and don't feel bad about it.

*(*GRETCHEN *cries.)*

REGINA: Come on. Here.

*(*REGINA *hands* GRETCHEN *a handkerchief.)*

(They watch for a bit.)

REGINA: Divorce is an interesting choice. Retrofitting some flaws into your perfect image in his head was a little challenging. I might have gone for a tragic death.

GRETCHEN: And have him pining for the memory of me for the rest of his life? No thanks. He needs to get to the point where he's ready for the next thing. Meet someone new. I actually asked Cindy if she was interested in meeting a good man.

REGINA: Did you?

GRETCHEN: It was meant to be a joke. I instantly regretted saying it, but she was intrigued. She said maybe she'll ask him out next time the Indigo Girls were playing a gig. *(She shrugs.)*

REGINA: It looks different from this side of the veil, doesn't it?

GRETCHEN: It's awful. I don't know how you can even watch this. People being led around like pets on invisible leashes.

REGINA: Even though you know it's for the better? You designed this endgame for him, invisible leash and all.

(A long silence)

REGINA: Speaking of which, now that your husband has been sorted out, there is the matter of what's to become of you.

GRETCHEN: What do you mean? You take your crap out and send me on my way. I thought that's what the agreement was.

REGINA: That certainly is one possibility.

*(*REGINA *moves to* GRETCHEN *and takes her by the chin.* GRETCHEN *is confused and recoils.)*

REGINA: I don't like it though. You have far too much potential.

GRETCHEN: Don't. Whatever you're thinking. Don't.

REGINA: You don't even want to consider what I might have to say?

GRETCHEN: If it means messing around with my head more, then no. I'm not going to sign on for another trophy wife stint.

REGINA: That's not what I was going to offer. My offer would be much more interesting.

GRETCHEN: I don't want to hear it.

REGINA: Very well. As you wish.

*(*GRETCHEN *and* REGINA *go on and watch offstage for a while. Eventually* GRETCHEN *snaps.)*

GRETCHEN: Okay, fine. What's the deal?

REGINA: I'd like for you to consider a possiblity. You see, I've been heading this company for quite a while. This body, though it's served me well, is starting to slow down a bit. We fix heads but bodies are another story. They age, they break. It's very inconvenient. I'm beginning to look for a successor is the point.

GRETCHEN: All right. What does that have to do with me?

REGINA: After you're done with your current situation, what would you think about leading this company?

GRETCHEN: Me? Lead LifeEnhanced?

REGINA: Yes.

GRETCHEN: I'm totally unqualified.

REGINA: We'll make you qualified. Technically, it'll be your body and the Gretchen persona augmented by my current relevant memories, abilities and settings. Essentially everything vital that's in my head can be transferred to you in the space of a weekend.

GRETCHEN: You want to…inhabit me?

REGINA: It's hard to explain. We'll use your general demeanor and personality but bounded by the hard knowledge contained within me, the mental governors which guide me to make appropriate decisions for the company. The result will be something of a synthesis between us. *(Pause)* Don't look so shocked. One of the issues we have is that we lack the vocabulary to adequately discuss what it is we're doing right now with the outside world. It'll take time for people to really understand.

GRETCHEN: I certainly don't.

REGINA: Think about it, love. Who is Gretchen Van der Pool? Some construct made out of echoes of other people housed in a body vacated by it's previous tenant. Who am I? Not too far removed from you, to be honest. I was a mere vice president who stepped forward when they decided they needed a friendly face to sell this service to the public. I would become what the company needed for a time, I would sacrifice parts of myself for a time, and in return I would be well compensated.

GRETCHEN: And what about you? Or her? How do you- Are there two people inside you?

REGINA: There are a multitude of people inside every person. Lovers, fighters, thinkers, doers. They come out as needed for the situation at hand. You realize this when you work in our line of business.

GRETCHEN: What will happen to the employee who… whose body you occupy? What happens to her when you leave?

REGINA: I'm so flattered that you care, my dear. She's still in here. And when I move on her personality will be restored and she'll be left with one hell of a golden parachute.

GRETCHEN: And you can just divorce yourself from… her? Just like that?

REGINA: Sure. I'll be elsewhere, and she'll remember her time with me, but she'll be more than content to ride off into the sunset with her generous 401K. Knowing her, she'll spend her days painting objectively horrible seascapes in a beachfront bungalow. And she'll be very happy doing so. That can be you in twelve to fifteen years. If you want to give Crystal Schenkman the best possible ending, you'll let me occupy her head for a little bit.

GRETCHEN: Why me?

REGINA: You're highly compatible to the process. Not everyone is but you're a natural. You're the right age, the right look. You present well. You'll wear the part well. You're good raw material. We recognized it then, and we've been proven right. Having you as a client all these years means that we have a good inventory of your current capabilities, and your potential capabilities. And you're available. Frankly it'd be a shame to waste you by having you go back to a life of working the register at a Starbucks or something.

GRETCHEN: Listen, this has been a lot to digest. I'll…I have to think about it before I decide.

REGINA: Yes, well technically, you won't be deciding.

GRETCHEN: Oh, no. No. Don't do this to Crystal!

REGINA: I'm sorry, but you know constructs can't give consent well enough to satisfy our ethics department.

GRETCHEN: You have an ethics department? Really?

REGINA: Of course. We want to push the boundaries, but we need to know where the boundaries are. There's no technical reason I can't force this upon you and make you think it was your idea. There's no technical reason I can't make twenty copies of my personality and install them into twenty different people. But we are sensitive to how things appear to those on the outside. It will take a while for ethics to catch up to the science.

GRETCHEN: Then why even ask me? Why not wait to talk to Crystal?

REGINA: Because then Crystal wouldn't get the benefit of your opinion. Remember all those questionnaires she filled out? Her choices and desires and wants? That's you. You're her fantasy of a perfect woman. Smart, composed, thoughtful. Surprisingly resourceful. You're someone she trusts and will listen to. Crystal will remember this conversation after we take the implants out, how it made you feel, what you ultimately decide is best. Whatever your opinion of the offer, I highly doubt that Crystal would ignore your counsel.

*(*GRETCHEN *struggles with all of this new information.)*

GRETCHEN: I need to know that this decision you're asking Crystal to make will be made entirely of her own free will.

REGINA: Of course. We will have as clear and transparent a process as possible.

GRETCHEN: If we do this—and I'm not saying we will— We need an outside observer to watch every interaction.

REGINA: That will be fine. Do you want Cindy?

GRETCHEN: Not her. You've been inside her brain. I want Ted to do it. I want him watching over every exchange. You…haven't done anything to him without him knowing it, have you?

REGINA: Please. We take no blame for the mind of Ted Naughton.

(That manages to get a brief laugh out of GRETCHEN.*)*

REGINA: It sounds like you may have made a decision or two.

*(*GRETCHEN *sighs. They exit.)*

Interlude 6
Gretchen's Transformation

(Darkness. Beeping and breathy whirring. Then the SURGEONS'S *voices.)*

SURGEON 1: ...58...59...60. All signs are stable. We can begin.

SURGEON 2: Alright, this is a new one. Reimplementation of the Gretchen Warner persona along with aspects of the Regina Hastings persona.

SURGEON 1: This one's gonna be interesting.

SURGEON 2: Let's begin.

Epilogue:
Gretchen's talk

(The same Tech Talk conference stage as RICH *presented at earlier. The* CONFERENCE HOST *is there.)*

CONFERENCE HOST: Ladies and gentlemen, please welcome CEO of LifeEnhanced, Gretchen Van der Pool!

*(*GRETCHEN *strides forth. She has* REGINA*'s self-possession and confidence now, and commands the stage.)*

GRETCHEN: Thank you, thank you all. When I first took leadership at LifeEnhanced, just over a decade ago, it was a business that, despite its promise, was on quite precarious ground. While people were happy to give themselves a new skill or improvement now and again, the full scope of what we could do was going to be unsettling to the public at large, and we knew it. People at that time were not comfortable with the idea that they could artificially remake themselves, remix themselves. It was something we had not publicized, because we feared the blowback. What does it mean to strive, to struggle, to live if we could remake ourselves to our own desires and specfications? It was a taboo subject long after it was clear that it was technologically viable and economically profitable. Was the world ready for this fundamental shift in the understanding of what it means to be human?

(Lights up on TED, *drinking alone. He looks unhappy and frazzled.)*

GRETCHEN: If you were sad, frustrated, unlucky or just had some deficiency you couldn't address by willpower, self-help, or gumption, were you fated to live your life that way? Or could you come to us for a helping hand? In recent years many industries were "disrupted" by new technologies. Television, banking, news media. Well we came along and "disrupted" the business of living.

As it happens, most of the world was ready for it. After we famously "came out" five years ago and unveiled the full scope of our services, there was a predictable firestorm of protests, lawsuits, reactionary laws, and controversy. We have survived the challenges, we have won almost every court case and beaten back the attempts to pass overintrusive regulation. We have given the people the services they desire, the lives they deserve,

(Lights up on RICH, *walking up to a door and knocking. He holds flowers.* CINDY *opens the door. They introduce each other, exchange a handshake and a polite kiss on the cheek. They begin their date.)*

GRETCHEN: The undeniable benefits of our services has been our best argument. Today any adult over the age of eighteen can walk into one of our clinics and improve their life. More than that, you can be more than just one person. You don't have to live your life in a little box anymore. You can be all business four days a week, then flip a switch and be someone else entirely for the other three.

(Lights up on REGINA, *in a bohemian pair of shorts, T-shirt, and sunhat, painting an objectively terrible seascape, and smiling.)*

GRETCHEN: My predecessor had to arrange her exit in secret, as very few knew exactly how enhanced she was during her term. Today, I can proudly disclose my real life story to the world. How I was born one person, chose to become another to make someone else happy, then chose to become another person again to take advantage of an opportunity, and I now can see the day in my future when I can lay down my responsilities to someone whom I know beyond a shadow of a doubt to be exactly as capable as me. On that day I can become, once again, wholly myself while someone else takes up the mantle of the leader of LifeEnhanced.

And on that day, I will ask myself what I want to do with the rest of my life. It's the same question that anyone has to answer every day. Even you, whether you want to admit it or not.

Thank you.

END OF PLAY

www.ingramcontent.com/pod-product-compliance
Lightning Source LLC
LaVergne TN
LVHW020657100826
845148LV00012B/2533

* 9 7 8 0 8 8 1 4 5 9 8 1 4 *